THE POWER OF JESUS

The Power
of Jesus

Nick Aiken

with illustrations
by Taffy

Series Editor: James Jones

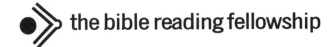 the bible reading fellowship

Text copyright Nick Aiken © 1993
Illustrations copyright Taffy © 1993

The author asserts the moral right
to be identified as the author of this work

Published by
The Bible Reading Fellowship
Peter's Way
Sandy Lane West
Oxford
OX4 5HG
ISBN 0 7459 2574 X
Albatross Books Pty Ltd
PO Box 320
Sutherland
NSW 2232
Australia
ISBN 0 7324 0760 5

First edition 1993

Acknowledgments
Scriptures quoted from the Good News Bible
published by The Bible Societies/HarperCollins
Publishers Ltd., UK © American Bible Society, 1966,
1971, 1976, 1992, with permission.

Material from The Alternative Service Book 1980 is
copyright © and reproduced by kind permission of
the Central Board of Finance of the Church of England.

The prayers in sections 16 and 18 are taken from
Prayers for Teenagers, HarperCollins

Extract 'Here and There' in section 14 by permission of
Chansitor Publications Ltd.

A catalogue record for this book is available
from the British Library

Printed and bound in Malta

By the same author:

Working with Teenagers
Prayers for Teenagers
More Prayers for Teenagers
Being Confirmed
Youthbuilders
Day Trips to Heaven (editor)
Big Ideas for Small Youth Groups (editor)
Your Life God's Way (editor)
Creative Ideas for Youth Evangelism (editor)
Available from HarperCollins

Contents

1

A celebration

Read John 2:1–4

Two days later there was a wedding in the town of Cana in Galilee. Jesus' mother was there, and Jesus and his disciples had also been invited to the wedding. When the wine had given out, Jesus' mother said to him, 'They have no wine left.' 'You must not tell me what to do,' Jesus replied. 'My time has not yet come.'

A wedding is a great occasion. It is an opportunity for family and friends to celebrate. It can be extremely nerve-racking for the bride and groom, but it will be a day they will never forget.

In Jesus' time weddings were very different from the way they are today. The groom would proceed to the house of the bride and then they would both walk back to the groom's house. However, this was not just a quiet walk. It was accompanied by celebrations and music and if it happened at night there would be a spectacular torchlight procession.

When the couple arrived at the groom's house, the reception would take place with food and wine. Sometimes the party would last for a number of days. If you were not careful you could run out of food or wine. And this was exactly what happened at the reception that Jesus was invited to.

As you can guess, all the celebrations could have come to a halt which would have been a disaster. So Jesus intervened and saved the party.

Write down any other events that families celebrate:

. . . .

. . . .

. . . .

. . . .

come for a reason to show people the way to God.

At the wedding Jesus was obviously aware that his special mission was just beginning. He knew that people would start looking at him. He wanted them to see beyond him to the Father who sent him. That is why he did these miracles: to show us that God was working through him.

Write down some of the special events that the Church celebrates throughout the year. What are they about?

. . . .

. . . .

. . . .

. . . .

Heavenly Father, thank you that we can see you at work through Jesus. Thank you that through his presence you added to the fun of the party.
Amen.

Jesus was aware that he had a special mission from God, this is why he said, 'My time has not yet come.' Jesus had

2
Family affairs

In the space draw your family tree. Make sure you list of all your parents, grandparents and brothers and sisters. Put as much detail on your tree as you are able. If you are in a group show each other your results.

At the wedding in Cana, it was Mary who asked Jesus to help:

When the wine had given out, Jesus' mother said to him, 'They have no wine left.' 'You must not tell me what to do,' Jesus replied. 'My time has not yet come.' Jesus' mother then told the servants, 'Do whatever he tells you.'

John 2:3–5

This seems as if Jesus was being rude to his Mum. But Mary was not offended by what Jesus said. Jesus was trying to point out that things were changing and something special was going to happen to him.

Mary obviously realized that Jesus was special and that he had extraordinary power. She knew this because of the special way in which Jesus was born. A messenger from God came to say that though she was a virgin she was to have a baby. This shocked Mary, but before he was born she knew he would be different.

If you are in a group, or working by yourself, put together details of the Christmas story by seeing how much you can remember of the events. If you need to check it out look at the beginning of Luke's Gospel at chapter 1, verses 26–56 and chapter 2, verses 1–21.

Jesus was also part of a family. Mary and Joseph were his parents and he had brothers and sisters. Because Mary was a very special person, the New Testament tells us far more about her than any other member of Jesus' family.

. . . .

. . . .

. . . .

Your parents are separating

. . . .

. . . .

. . . .

Mary trusted that her son Jesus would know what to do. That is why she told the servants, 'Do whatever he tells you.' Mary is a good example to us. She put her faith and trust in Jesus. She knew that he could be relied on. She may not have known what Jesus was about to do, but she knew that whatever he should say or do ought to be obeyed. Mary was very wise.
In what ways can you trust and put your faith in Jesus—at school or at home or with your friends? What would Jesus want you to do in the situations you find yourself in? Think of a situation where you have conflict at either home or school and write down how you think Jesus would handle the situation. Here are a number of suggestions that may help you to think:
Your best friend is found cheating

. . . .

. . . .

. . . .

Someone in your class is being bullied

. . . .

. . . .

. . . .

You are moving to a new school

. . . .

. . . .

. . . .

Dear God, when life is difficult and things don't work out help me to put my trust in you. Help me not to forget you when I feel down but to rely on the strength that you give.

THINGS WILL NEVER BE THE SAME!

3

A lot of things change. Caterpillars change into butterflies, seeds change into flowers, babies eventually change into adults and peace can change into war. Some changes happen naturally, but others happen because you and I have the power to change things.

List three things below which you would like to change:

1 . . . .

2 . . . .

3 . . . .

Now list three things which you personally have the power to change:

1 . . . .

2 . . . .

3 . . . .

Are any of the things in your two lists the same? If you are in a group, discuss the things that you have each listed down. Talk about what things you personally can change, what things the group may be able to change and what things are beyond your power to change. If you are on your own, put a star beside any of the items on your list that are the same.

All change!

Read John 2:6–10

The Jews have rules about ritual washing, and for this purpose six stone water jars were there, each one large enough to hold about a hundred litres. Jesus said to the servants, 'Fill these jars with water.' They filled them to the brim, and then he told them, 'Now draw some water out and take it to the man in charge of the feast.' They took him the water, which now had turned into wine, and he tasted it. He did not know were this wine had come from (but, of course, the servants who had drawn out the water knew); so he called the bridegroom and said to him, 'Everyone else serves the best wine first, and the after the guests have had plenty to drink, he serves the ordinary wine. But you have kept the best wine until now!'

THE GOOD NEWS IS YOU'LL BE ABLE TO FLY - THE BAD NEWS IS - YOU'LL ONLY LIVE FOR TWENTY FOUR HOURS!

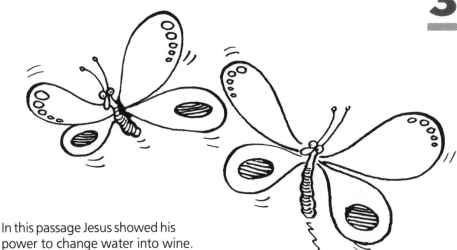

In this passage Jesus showed his power to change water into wine. Why do you think Jesus changed the water to wine. Was it for fun or was there a reason behind it? Was it because:

☐ He was too lazy to go to the local wine shop

☐ He thought his own wine would be better

☐ He wanted to show them how powerful he was

☐ He wanted to make them think

☐ He knew the local wine shop would be closed

☐ He wanted them see beyond the miracle to something of greater importance

Tick the ones you think are right. What other situations or people did Jesus change? For example, Jesus changed a storm on the Sea of Galilee into calm. List two others that you can think of:

1 ....

2 ....

Although water is important, it is very ordinary. You simply turn the tap and out it flows. Or in Jesus' time you would go to the nearest well. But wine is special. It has a rich taste.
Jesus had the power to change water into wine. He also has the power to change our life from something ordinary to something special. He wants to change us from being orphans who do not know God to children who know that they have a Father who loves them. What a great change!

Father God, thank you that you have the power to change things. Please help me to allow you to change my life. Amen.

4

Everything has to start at the beginning. For example the alphabet starts with A and numbers start with 1. A race will begin with, 'Ready, steady, go!' and a football match with a whistle.

Here is a list of different things. What kind of starts do they begin with?

A school sports day

. . . .

A computer game

. . . .

A Church service

. . . .

A school lesson

. . . .

A life

. . . .

A friendship

. . . .

Read John 2:11

Jesus performed this first miracle in Cana in Galilee; there he revealed his glory, and his disciples believed in him.

This was the first miracle that Jesus did and the writer tells us exactly where it happened . . . in Cana in Galilee. This miracle marked the start of Jesus' public life. From there he went about teaching and doing many more miracles over the next three years. But Jesus was not a magician. He did not perform tricks just to amuse people. He worked miracles because he wanted to show people that something special had just begun. The special

Just for starters

We all see miracles around us every day. Most miracles we miss because we take them for granted. What miracles do we see in creation and what do they tell us about God?

A baby being born . . . .

news was that God—in the person of Jesus—had come down to earth to show us how much he loves us. What great news! No wonder the disciples got so excited.

A high mountain . . . .

The miracles that Jesus did showed his glory—the power that Jesus had because of the important person he was.

A tiny creature . . . .

In the verse above it mentions that three things happened. First, that he turned water into wine. What are the other two things?

The stars at night . . . .

1 He turned water into wine.

2 . . . .

3 . . . .

Miracles show us

1 The power of Jesus

2 That God loves us

3 That God wants to be our friend

Lord Jesus, thank you for the start you made in Cana. Thank you for the start you've made in my life. Thank you for the new start I've made in following you. Help me to keep our friendship alive. Amen.

5

Jesus' reputation spread throughout all of Israel. People heard that he did miracles and healed the sick. Amazing! On one occasion an official rushed to see him because his son was terribly ill. He knew that unless he got help his son would die. A desperate situation.

The man in this story was more than just an ordinary official. He was connected to the royal court and was a man of importance. Capernaum was about twenty miles from Cana so it would have taken three or four hours by horse or longer if he had to walk. Jesus at first told the man off. What did he say to him? Write it down in the space opposite in your own style.

Here's the story:

Then Jesus went back to Cana in Galilee, where he had turned the water into wine. A government official was there whose son was ill in Capernaum. When he heard that Jesus had come from Judaea to Galilee, he went to him and asked him to go to Capernaum and heal his son, who was about to die. Jesus said to him, 'None of you will ever believe unless you see miracles and wonders.' 'Sir,' replied the official, 'come with me before my child dies.' Jesus said to him, 'Go, your son will live!' The man believed Jesus' words and went.

John 4:46–50

Trust and

It is important to ask for God's help when we're in a difficult situation. It may not always work out the way we want. But the important thing is that we trust God and leave the situation with him.

Note down one thing that has gone well during the past week. Then something that has gone wrong.

Right . . . .

. . . .

Wrong. . . . .

. . . .

obey

Jesus did not want people to believe in him just because he had the power to do spectacular things. We should not believe in God just because we want him to do things for us. The main reason we believe in God is because he is God!
The official knew that Jesus could help and that he had the power to do so. So when Jesus said, 'Go, your son will live!' he took Jesus at his word and trusted him. He accepted what Jesus said although he did not see any sign or miracle. He trusted and obeyed.

If you are in a group, take turns in mentioning what has happened to each other. If you are alone, quietly tell God about it and ask for his help.

Lord help me to trust and obey you. I know that you are God. Help me when things don't work out the way I want and life is difficult. Amen

CAPERNAUM
20 MILES.

Here's a list of the types of people who give orders. On a scale of 0-10 circle the number as to how much you would respect their orders (0 = no respect, 10 = great respect).

Policeman
0 1 2 3 4 5 6 7 8 9 10
Headteacher
0 1 2 3 4 5 6 7 8 9 10
Prefect
0 1 2 3 4 5 6 7 8 9 10
Traffic Warden
0 1 2 3 4 5 6 7 8 9 10
Politician
0 1 2 3 4 5 6 7 8 9 10
Referee
0 1 2 3 4 5 6 7 8 9 10
Youthclub Leader
0 1 2 3 4 5 6 7 8 9 10

What was the order that Jesus give in this passage? Look again at John 4:46–53 and we shall continue the story from the last session:

On his way home his servants met him with news, 'Your boy is going to live!' He asked them what time it was when his son got better, and they answered, 'It was one o'clock yesterday afternoon when the fever left him.' Then the father remembered that it was at that very hour when Jesus had told him, 'Your son will live.'

John 4:51–53

Jesus' words were very powerful. He had the power to say that someone would be well and they got better. But then God often said powerful things. In the book of Genesis at the creation of the world God said, 'Let there be light'—and light appeared. But people who give orders do so because of who they are and what they are. For example the words of the national team coach for the Olympics are important because they have the power to include or exclude people from the team.

Go back to the list of the people who give orders and now put them in a list of importance, number 1 being the most important.

The official recognized that Jesus was someone special and he knew because of the many other people he healed that he was a powerful person. So, when Jesus gave him his order to go home because his son would live, he knew that he should obey.

The words of Jesus are powerful because of who he is and what he is. We as Christians should respect his words and follow the commands he gives us.

Powerful words

Heavenly Father, thank you that you are a God who speaks and things happen. Help us to be aware of how important you are and obey your orders and instructions.

7

 Read John 4:53

| *So he and all his family believed*

It was very difficult to come into contact with Jesus and not be affected by him. After meeting Jesus, things would never be the same again for this family. They all believed in him. Why? Because they saw the power of God working through him. You may say, 'It was all right for them, they had direct contact with Jesus in a miraculous way. It was easy for them to believe.' But you and I also can see the power of God working through Jesus in many different ways. Let's look at the evidence:

1. **The Bible.** It tells all about God. What he is like and what he does. All the evidence is there. Page after page is filled with examples to show us that God is alive and real.

All . . .
yes all
believed!

2. **The Church.** Can all these millions of Christians be wrong? Can all the Christians who have believed in Jesus over the past two thousand years and who achieved so much to change things for the good be wrong? How was it that Jesus influenced and changed so many peoples lives? Answer: because it's true.

Make a list, below, of all the things you have eaten during the day. Then list all the different types of people that would have been involved in getting that food to you. If you are in a group compare your lists.

3. **Creation.** Look at the world around you. Look at the beauty of nature. Think of the amazing design of the human brain. It takes more faith to believe it just happened than to believe there is a God who created and keeps the world going.

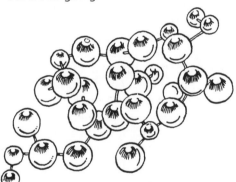

With everything you eat or drink many people will have a part to play in getting it to your table. But it was God who started off the process.

The official and his family had already seen the power of God all around them. God had created the world, had given them a home and food. He had given them a son. Sadly they believed only when Jesus made him better again, but God had already been doing things for them long before Jesus arrived on the scene.

4. **Science.** Science has not disproved that God exists. Science describes how things happen. The Bible tells us why things happen. A great many scientists believe in God. In fact in an American opinion poll it was discovered that at least seven out of every ten scientists believed in God.

Dear Father God you have done so much for each of us. Help us to see all that you have done and grow in our belief in you. Amen.

8

Read John 4:54

This was the second miracle that Jesus performed after coming from Judaea to Galilee.

Jesus did lots of miracles. Without looking at the rest of this book can you list some of the other miracles that you remember:

. . . .

. . . .

. . . .

. . . .

The writer of the Gospel was very concerned to write down the details of what Jesus said and did in a correct account. We could list on a very large sheet of paper all the miracles that Jesus did. We could also list all the stories that he told. We could then go on to mention all the people who were affected by Jesus' words and miracles. All three lists would be very impressive pieces of evidence as to the importance of Jesus.

BUT the problem with believing that Jesus did these miracles is that we don't see these things happening today. It's led some people—even Christians—to doubt that Jesus really did them. But it all depends on what your starting point is.

1. If you think that Jesus was just a very kind person that it's hard to believe that these miracles are true.

2. If you think that Jesus could have been the special agent of the Creator of the Universe then it's possible to imagine that he would have had some supernatural power.

If you take the first view then you'll try to explain away the miracle stories. If you take the second view then your mind can stay open to the possibility that these things really happened.

Jesus was unique—no one has said or done such remarkable things. All the evidence we have is based on reliable records of the Gospels. The writers of all four Gospels tell the stories of Jesus' words and actions and each gives us a different picture of the events. They put it in different ways. But they all agree that he performed miracles and rose from the dead.

The evidence helps us to believe in Jesus, and the more of the evidence we examine, the more it helps us believe in God.

Dear Lord, we thank you for giving us the Bible. It shows us how to believe in you. Help us to get to know the Bible better. Amen.

The evidence
is reliable

9

Read John 5:1–9

After this, Jesus went to Jerusalem for a religious festival. Near the Sheep Gate in Jersalem there is a pool with five porches; in Hebrew it is called Bethzatha. A large crowd of sick people were lying in the porches—the blind, the lame, and the paralysed. A man was there who had been ill for thirty-eight years. Jesus saw him lying there, and he knew that the man had been ill for such a long time; so he asked him, 'Do you want to get well?' The sick man answered, 'Sir, I have no one here to put me in the pool when the water is stirred up; while I am trying to get in, somebody else gets there first.' Jesus said to him, 'Get up, pick up your mat, and walk.' Immediately the man got well; he picked up his mat and started walking. The day this happened was a Sabbath.

Today the religious festivals we keep are Christmas and Easter. Jesus was a Jew and so always kept the religious festivals. At the beginning of this story he was in Jerusalem for one of them. Jerusalem is one of the oldest cities in the world.

If you are in a group, find out what cities each member of the group has been to. Then discuss what are some of the common sights you see in a city. What are some of the good things you see and what are some of the bad things?

Good sights: ....

. . . .

. . . .

. . . .

. . . .

. . . .

. . . .

Bad sights: ....

. . . .

. . . .

. . . .

. . . .

. . . .

. . . .

. . . .

Help is at hand

In this city there was a large crowd of sick people sitting around a pool. They were there because they were ill and hoped that when the waters stirred the first one to jump into the pool would be cured. Whether anyone had been cured this way it does not say, but this is what the people there believed. People often associate water with making people better. Sometimes when you are very sick all you can drink is water. But Jesus does not offer to hang around and help him when the waters stir. He just says, 'Get up, pick up your mat, and walk.'

The power of Jesus' words is amazing. This man had been lame for 38 years. Jesus took pity and helped him. The man did not even know who Jesus was. This passage shows us that God is prepared to help those who don't even know anything about him.

In many of our cities there are young people sleeping rough. They've run away. Many of them feel that nobody cares about them. Jesus loves them as much as he loved the crippled man. But it's hard for these young people to believe that anybody loves them, let alone God. Talk about this with your friends at church and with the leader of your youth group: how can the church prove to these young people that God really does love them?

Dear God, thank you that you freely offer your love to us. You are always willing to listen and help. Take care of our cities especially those young people who are poor, sick and those who are homeless. Let your example inspire us to help those in need.
Amen.

HOMELESS

10

Don't miss the point

Read John 5:10–13

> So the Jewish authorities told the man who had been healed, 'This is the Sabbath, and it is against our Law for you to carry your mat.' He answered, 'The man who made me well told me to pick up my mat and walk.' They asked him, 'Who is the man who told you to do this?' But the man who had been healed did not know who Jesus was, for there was a crowd in that place, and Jesus had slipped away.

What day did this miracle take place on?

. . . .

What was so important about this day?

. . . .

. . . .

When someone is ill you might send them a 'Get well' card. You may even visit them in hospital if the illness is serious. When they get better, everyone is happy. However this man had been ill for 38 years and then suddenly Jesus made him well again. This was a cause for celebration. You would have thought that the religious authorities would have been very pleased for the man. So how did they completely miss the point? Well, the Sabbath, which is the Jewish day of rest, is supposed to be a day in which you do no work. So the authorities made various rules as to what you should and should not do on the Sabbath. As far as they were concerned, carrying your mat was work! Talk about missing the point by a mile.

People are more important than religious rules and regulations. This man who had been so ill for so long, Jesus had healed. And yet all they were concerned about was the rules. Sad isn't it?

Sometimes things get in our way of seeing what's most important. We may think that the religious authorities were stupid. But what are some of the things that stop us from seeing what's most important? You might think about possessions or pressure from your friends.

List them here:

Lord, sometimes I get lost and forget about you. Help me to see clearly all the good things you have done and thank you for them. Amen.

. . . .

. . . .

. . . .

. . . .

Which of the things you have listed above get in the way all the time and which some of the time? Put **A** or **S** against each item for all or some. If you are in a group, discuss your results with your friends.

11

Everyone knows what red means at traffic lights. Stop! If people ignored the red lights it would cause chaos. You may know of cases were someone has driven through a red light and the result has been an accident.

In this passage Jesus told the man who he had healed to stop!

> Afterwards, Jesus found him in the temple and said:
> 'Listen, you are well now; so stop sinning or something worse may happen to you.'

John 5:14

Jesus was pointing out that sin makes things go wrong. For example hatred causes violence, greed causes theft, selfishness causes loneliness. The man whom Jesus had healed had been given the power for a new start. But Jesus did not want him to spoil it by doing things wrong. So he said stop. Turn over a new leaf. You've been made physically better now live your life in a better way. Jesus gives us all the power to stop, turn and go in a new, better direction. Look at the two lists and tick the things you think you should stop doing and the things you should start doing.

Stop being:
- ☐ Unkind
- ☐ Dishonest
- ☐ Selfish
- ☐ Greedy
- ☐ Stubborn
- ☐ Impatient

Start being:
- ☐ Honest
- ☐ Understanding
- ☐ Kind
- ☐ Generous
- ☐ Trustworthy
- ☐ Forgiving

Dear Lord, help me to stop when I know I'm going the wrong way and to start going your way. Amen.

P.S. Choose one from each list to work on in the coming week.

12

Read John 5:15–18

Then the man left and told the Jewish authorities that it was Jesus who had healed him. So they began to persecute Jesus, because he had done this healing on a Sabbath. Jesus answered them, 'My Father is always working, and I too must work.' This saying made the Jewish authorities all the more determined to kill him; not only had he broken the Sabbath law, but he had said that God was his own Father and in this way had made himself equal with God.

Being a follower of Jesus is not easy. You may be teased or bullied at times for what you believe. Jesus found it tough going. People missed the point and did not like what he said and did. Eventually the authorities put him to death.

The going gets tough

SELFISH-NESS

TEMPTATION

BULLYING

In what ways is being a Christian difficult? You may find it hard at home or at school or among your friends. Note down some of the difficulties of following Jesus.

at home ....

....

....

at school ....

....

....

with friends ....

....

....

If you are in a group compare your notes and find out ways which you can help each other.

Heavenly Father, being a Christian is sometimes very difficult. It's not easy to be honest. Give me strength when others hassle me for my faith. Help me to remember that Jesus did not give up when things got tough. And when I fail, forgive me. Amen

P.S. Out of the lists, what do you think is the most difficult? Write down below how Jesus would have reacted if he were in your shoes.

....

....

....

....

....

LUST

REED

13

The fourth sign or miracle that Jesus did which showed his power was the feeding of the five thousand. The story begins in John chapter 6:

After this, Jesus went across Lake Galilee (or, Lake Tiberias, as it is also called). A large crowd followed him, because they had seen his miracles of healing those who were ill. Jesus went up a hill and sat down with his disciples. The time for the Passover Festival was near. Jesus looked round and saw that a large crowd was coming to him, so he asked Philip, 'Where can we buy enough food to feed all these people?' (He said this to test Philip; actually he already knew what he would do.) Philip answered, 'For everyone to have even a little, it would take more than two hundred silver coins to buy enough bread.

John 6:1–7

All of us worry about things. It's a very natural thing to do. Note down the things that you are worried about in the space below. It may concern school, home or friends. You will not have to show this to anyone else.

Sometimes being worried achieves nothing. It just makes you feel bad. All you can see is the problem. The answer is nowhere in sight.

Jesus presented Philip with a problem, not because he wanted to tease him, but because he wanted to find out whether Philip had realized that Jesus could handle the situation. Philip did not know the answer but Jesus did.

Stop worrying

'Where can we buy enough food to feed all these people?' Philip, however, could not see the answer. What was his reply to Jesus? Write it down below:

....

....

....

The disciples did not have two hundred silver coins to buy bread. (One silver coin was the day's pay of a farm worker.) So two hundred silver coins was a lot of money. Jesus asked this question to see if Philip knew the answer. But Philip had not realized that Jesus had the power to provide the answer. Philip had not yet discovered that Jesus could be trusted.

The answer was not in having enough money. The answer was to trust Jesus and to trust God.

A Christian, George Herbert, once said, 'God provides for him who trusts.' another Christian said, 'You may trust the Lord too little, but you can never trust him too much.'

. . **trust**

Lord, when life is difficult help me to always trust you.
Amen.

14 Sharing

The story of the feeding of the five thousand occurs in all of the Gospels. What are the other three Gospels called?

1 ....

2 ....

3 ....

There is a story from Korea which tells of a warrior who died and went to heaven. When he arrived, the gatekeeper insisted that first he would take him on a tour of hell. When he got there he was astonished to see a large table piled high with wonderful food. Yet all the people in hell were starving. The warrior enquired of the gatekeeper why this was the case. He explained that everyone in hell had chopsticks five foot long which they had to hold at the end. The result was that no one could reach their mouth. The warrior agreed that this was indeed hell and asked to be taken back to heaven immediately. However when they arrived in heaven he was surprised to see a similar table again piled high with the most wonderful food. Yet the people in heaven looked happy and well fed. The warrior turned to the gatekeeper, 'No chopsticks?' 'Oh yes,' explained the gatekeeper. 'They are also five foot long and must be held at the end, but in heaven people have come to feed each other.'

John Hogan,
'Here and There'

In the Gospel the story continues:

Another of his disciples, Andrew, who was Simon Peter's brother, said, 'There is a boy here who has five loaves of barley bread and two fish. But they will certainly not be enough for all these people.'

John 6:8–9

In this miracle that Jesus did, a little that was shared for the benefit of others went further than anyone could have imagined. As we share what we have together, we show the power of God's love. We also show what heaven is like.

In the word box below there are eight words that all relate to sharing together and being friends. See if you can quickly find them all.

```
Q S C V B N Y I O C
P A T I E N C E Z A
A S X R Z M L P D R
Z G C H U D L O V E
X H D O L S W R E T
C J W N K P T I O P
V K Q E J F A I T H
B L Y S H U G H J K
L I S T E N I N G W
```

One Christian once said, 'Trust God for great things; with your five loaves and two fishes, He will show you a way to feed thousands.'

List the names of people who have influenced things for the better.

....

....

....

Dear God, take my life and let me help others. Help me to think not just of how I can help myself but how I can share with others. Amen.

15

Enough for everyone

 The story now changes from the disciples trying to solve the problem to what Jesus does.

'Make the people sit down,' Jesus told them. (There was a lot of grass there.) So all the people sat down; there were about five thousand men. Jesus took the bread, gave thanks to God, and distributed it to the people who were sitting there. He did the same with the fish, and they all had as much as they wanted. When they were all full, he said to his disciples, 'Gather the pieces left over; let us not waste any.' So they gathered them all up and filled twelve baskets with the pieces left over from the five barley loaves which the people had eaten.

John 6:10–13

This story reminds us of the communion service. We take and eat what has been offered to God. We each take a small piece and it goes around all the people gathered together. There is always enough for everybody.

It's a sign that with God there is always enough for everyone. No one will ever be denied his love. No one will be left out or told there is not enough. Sometimes we may discover at home or school that there is not enough of something. There may not be enough money to buy an item. There may not be enough books to go around all the class. Not having enough can at times cause hardship. But with God this is not the case. There is enough of his love for everyone.

When the bread and the wine have been offered to God we often use a difficult word to describe what has happened to it. The word in the circle:

The bread and the wine becomes for us the body and blood of Jesus. As Christians we believe that his body was broken and his blood shed for us. When we've received God's love through the bread and wine at communion we say together:

Almighty God, we thank you for feeding us with body and blood of your Son Jesus Christ. Through him we offer you our souls and bodies to be a living sacrifice. Send us out in the power of your Spirit to live and work to your praise and glory. Amen.

ASB

16
SPECIAL OFFER

This miracle that Jesus performed also shows us that Jesus has the power to supply our needs. He was not trying to establish the world's first fast food chain. Rather he was showing that he had something special to give and that he could meet people's needs. God can supply not just our physical needs but all that we need, body, mind and spirit. God invites us to come and receive what he alone can give.

Isaiah, one of the Old Testament prophets wrote:

The Lord says, 'Come, everyone who is thirsty—here is water! Come, you that have no money—buy corn and eat! Come! Buy wine and milk—it will cost you nothing! Why spend money on what does not satisfy? Why spend your wages and still be hungry? Listen to me and do what I say, and you will enjoy the best food of all. Listen now, my people, and come to me; come to me, and you will have life!'

Isaiah 55:1–3

Powerful words! You can imagine how popular a shop would be that sold all its goods for nothing. There would be queues every day stretching down the street! People would come for miles to take what is being given away. God is inviting us to take what you do not need money to buy. Unlike food which you eat and then are hungry again, this food satisfies. While food keeps our bodies going, this food gives life at a deeper level. And the person who has the power to feed five thousand also has the power from God to offer us life itself. Life of eternal value that goes on forever.

God gives us with this amazing invitation?

Here is a list of invitations you may receive. You may be very busy so list them according to importance. 1 being top priority and 5 being least important.

☐ Meeting a friend for coffee

☐ Going with a crowd to the cinema

☐ Being called to see your teacher

☐ Accepting an invitation from God

☐ Accepting a party invitation

Lord God, thank you for all your blessings; for life and health, for laughter and fun, for all our powers of mind and body, for our homes and health, for everything that is beautiful, good and true. Above all we thank you for giving your Son to be our Saviour and Friend. Amen.

17

We now come to the fifth sign in John's Gospel which shows Jesus' power: the incident of Jesus walking on water.

Read John 6:16–19

When evening came, Jesus' disciples went down to the lake, got into a boat, and went back across the lake towards Capernaum. Night came on, and Jesus still had not come to them. By then a strong wind was blowing and stirring up the water. The disciples had rowed about five or six kilometres when they saw Jesus walking on the water.

When the Queen attends special state functions she wears the royal crown. It shows everyone that she has been given the authority to rule as sovereign over this land.

Jesus walks on water

In the same way Jesus walking on water is a sign of his authority. He has power over everything. He has created the world and everything in it. The whole of creation responds to his command. His power is unlimited. There is nothing he cannot do.

Jesus walked on water to give the disciples a clearer idea of who he was. He did it, not to show off, but to help all his followers to understand his authority.

Write down the names of other people in our country have authority and then write what power goes with that position.

Name / Position   Power

. . . .

. . . .

. . . .

. . . .

In what ways should we obey Jesus' authority?

at home . . . .

. . . .

at school. . . . .

. . . .

with friends. . . . .

. . . .

Are there times when obeying Jesus' authority brings us in conflict with our parents, teachers or friends? If so, write down what you think you should do. If you are in a group discuss you answers together.

. . . .

. . . .

. . . .

. . . .

. . . .

. . . .

—BUT JESUS HAS TOLD ME TO DYE MY HAIR ORANGE!

Eternal Father, whose Son Jesus Christ ascended to the throne of heaven that he might rule over all things as Lord . . . bring the whole created order to worship at his feet; who is alive and reigns with you and the Holy Spirit, one God, now and for ever.

18
HELP... I'm afraid

The story continues...

... *when they saw Jesus walking on water, coming near the boat, and they were terrified.*

John 6:19

Stop for a moment and put yourself in the disciples' shoes. Note down what you would have felt seeing Jesus walking on water:

. . . .

. . . .

. . . .

. . . .

Jot down some of the things that have terrified you. Make a note beside them as to what your reaction was at the time.

. . . .

. . . .

. . . .

. . . .

The disciples were terrified at the sight of Jesus walking on water. They had not seen anything like this before. Their reaction was natural. If we saw something supernatural we'd probably be afraid.
Many young people play around with Ouijah boards, Tarot Cards and seances. What starts off as a game can

sometimes get very frightening. These things can put you in touch with a supernatural world of darkness. The Bible warns us against playing around with the supernatural.

Like the physical world which we can touch and see, the spiritual world is made up of light and darkness, the good and the bad. God is stronger than the power of evil. God is the only supernatural power that we should open our lives to.

Lord Jesus, Son of God, I open my life to you. I turn away from every bad influence. Lead me not into temptation and deliver me from evil. Amen.

A Christian once said, 'He who fears God need fear nothing else, and he who fears not God needs to fear everything else.'

19
Don't be afraid . . .

The disciples must have been very relieved to hear those words from Jesus. They were frightened because of the storm and by the sight of someone walking on water. On a number of occasions in the Bible, Jesus had to reassure the disciples by saying 'It's OK, I'm here.' Without him they would often become afraid and unsure of what to do. Then he would return and help them sort things out.

Can you remember getting lost when you were a child? It may have been in a busy supermarket or department store. You let go of your parent's hand and in the confusion you lost sight of them. Tears flowed, the crying began because you felt afraid. However,

when Mum or Dad appeared all was well and you felt safe again. But you do not need to be a child to feel afraid. When you're older things often go wrong. You're not sure what to do. You wish you had someone to turn to. The wonderful thing is that as a Christian we always have God to turn to. He is there in the easy and difficult times. Repeatedly in the Bible God reminds his people that he is with them. In fact, I've often wondered why God says so often that he his with us. I think it's because we are slow to listen and understand.

MUM!

it is I

As Christians we can overcome our fear by realizing God is with us.
In the space below write down your own prayer giving to God whatever you are worried about at the moment.

. . . .

. . . .

. . . .

. . . .

. . . .

. . . .

Thank you, Lord, for being there to help and comfort me. I know I can always trust you. If I'm in trouble, there you'll be. In every stage of living, Lord, you're always there to guide. Amen.

Now, imagine Jesus coming into the situation. Imagine what he would say to you and write it down below.

. . . .

. . . .

. . . .

. . . .

20

Safely

Read
John 6:21

> Then they willingly took him into the boat, and immediately the boat reached land at the place they were heading for.

St Paul realized this when he said:

You may have a lot of questions. Some of your questions may be so difficult no one can give you a good answer. Many of your questions may start with the word 'Why?' Why am I here? Why did this happen? Why is there so much suffering in the world? This story helps us to know that when we're overwhelmed with problems and question Jesus can be relied on to guide us safely through the chaos and confusion.

In this passage the disciples were caught in a storm. Things were getting rough. But as soon as Jesus got on board they arrived safely at their destination.

We too may feel tossed about with all sorts of questions and difficulties that will not go away. However, as Christians we know that in the end God will never let us go. Our plans for the future may go wrong. But we are assured that we will get to our final destination safely—heaven.

> No, in all these things we have complete victory through him who loved us! For I am certain that nothing can separate us from his love: neither death nor life, neither angels nor other heavenly rulers or powers, neither the present nor the future, neither the world above nor the world below—there is nothing in all creation that will ever be able to separate us from the love of God which is ours through Christ Jesus our Lord.
>
> Romans 8:37–39

Lord, times are difficult. I need to know that you are near, that you are watching over me and most of all that you love me. Please guide me in everything I say and do. Thank you. Amen.

Nothing can separate us from God's love. You may not be in a boat caught in a storm. At this moment you are probably sitting safely in a chair or on the floor. But, in the pictures of the four boats below, write the worst situations you could imagine yourself in. When you have done that, draw a cross over the top of the boat and the safety of dry land beside it.

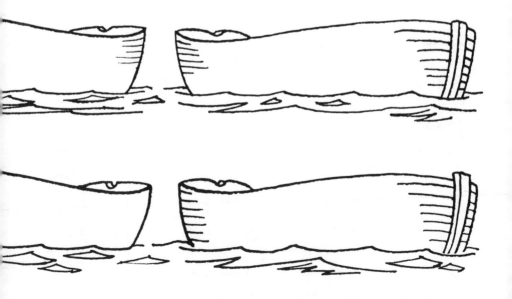

21

Difficult questions

 Read John 9:1–5

> *As Jesus walked along, he saw a man who had been born blind. His disciples asked him, 'Teacher, whose sin caused him to be born blind? Was it his own or his parents' sin?' Jesus answered, 'His blindness has nothing to do with his sins or his parents' sins. He is blind so that God's power might be seen at work in him. As long as it is day, we must keep on doing the work of him who sent me; night is coming when no one can work. While I am in the world, I am the light for the world.'*

In the times that the Bible was written, people thought that if you were ill or something went wrong you were being punished. So the disciples wanted to know whose fault it was that the man was born blind. Was it his or his parents'?

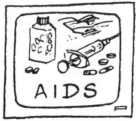

Things do go wrong for a reason. They are the result of a particular action. Think of some examples of the action you or someone took and the result that it had.

Action   Result

. . . .

. . . .

. . . .

However not everything goes wrong just because of something that happened: for example, an earthquake or a storm.
Can you think of any other examples?

. . . .

. . . .

. . . .

Even today when things go wrong we can think that God must be punishing us for something we've done.
All the religions in the world try to figure out why people suffer. It was Jesus, alone of all the religious leaders, who said quite clearly that suffering was NEVER a punishment from God. Christians see suffering in a new light:
1. When we suffer we remember that God too suffered on the cross.
2. God takes suffering and brings something good out of it. Through the suffering of Jesus on the cross he brought about the salvation of the world.

3. God promises to put an end to suffering one day. 'God will wipe away all tears from their eyes. There will be no more death, no more grief or crying or pain' (Revelation 21:4).

Lord, I believe in you;
the God who cries
the God who suffers
the God who brings good out of evil
the God who promises an end to
death, grief and pain. Lord, I belive
in you. Amen.

22

Read John 9:6–11

After he said this, Jesus spat on the ground and made some mud with the spittle; he rubbed the mud on the man's eyes and said, 'Go and wash your face in the Pool of Siloam.' (This name means 'Sent.') So the man went, washed his face, and came back seeing. His neighbours, then, and the people who had seen him begging before this, asked, 'Isn't this the man who used to sit and beg?' Some said, 'He is the one,' but others said, 'No he isn't; he just looks like him.' So the man himself said, 'I am the man.' 'How is it that you can now see?' they asked him. He answered, 'The man called Jesus made some mud, rubbed it on my eyes and told me to go to Siloam and wash my face. So I went, and as soon as I washed, I could see.'

In the Old Testament, the first part of the Bible, the giving of sight is something God himself does. This powerful sign that Jesus performs is therefore meant to show us that Jesus is the Son of God. He is able to do what God does and he is sent by him. The Gospels record that Jesus healed people in a variety of ways. The way he healed this man was different from the way he healed the official's son and the lame man. Jesus did not have a particular way of doing things, but treated people as individuals. So he healed people in different ways. The man who was healed simply described what happened. He followed Jesus' instructions and as a result he could see. The man could have ignored Jesus because he thought that no one had the power to give him back his sight.

God treats each of us as individuals. Look at the prints on your fingers. Take a very close look at them. Of all the billions of people in the world no one has a finger print like yours. Incredible isn't it? We are all different.

You are different from other people in lots of ways. Fill in the details below and if you are in a group compare what you have written down.

Date of birth.........................

Favourite food ....

Colour of eyes ....

Where you where born ....

Number of foreign countries you have

visited ....

Favourite music band ....

....

Favourite colour ....

Number of brothers and sisters ....

Lord, thank you that you have created each of us us as individuals. Thank you that even though we are different people you care about each one of us. Amen.

I can see!

The religious leaders decided to investigate further the case of the man born blind. They were not sure whether it was true. They were also trying to find out who this person Jesus really was:

Then they took to the Pharisees the man who had been blind. The day that Jesus made the mud and cured him of his blindness was a Sabbath. The

Pharisees, then, asked the man again how he had received his sight. He told them, 'He put some mud on my eyes; I washed my face, and now I can see.' Some of the Pharisees said, 'The man who did this cannot be from God, for he does not obey the Sabbath law.' Others, however, said, 'How could a man who is a sinner perform such miracles as these?' And there was a division among them. So the Pharisees asked the man once more, 'You say he cured you of your blindness—well, what do you say about him?' 'He is a prophet,' the man answered . . . A second time they called back the man who had been born blind, and said to him, 'Promise before God that you will tell the truth! We know that this man who cured you is a sinner.' 'I do not know if he is a sinner or not,' the man replied. 'One thing I do know: I was blind, and now I see.' 'What did he do to you?' they asked. 'How did he cure you of your blindness?' 'I have already told you,' he answered, 'and you would not listen. Why do you want to hear it again? Maybe you, too, would like to be his disciples?' They cursed him and said, 'You are that fellow's disciple; but we are Moses' disciples. We know

Profile

Jesus...

	YES	NO
COMMANDED ARMIES	☐	☑
POWERFUL RULER	☐	☑
WROTE BOOKS	☐	☑
EXPLORER	☐	☑
LIVED A LONGTIME	☐	☑
MADE A FORTUNE	☐	☑

that God spoke to Moses; as for that fellow, however, we do not even know where he comes from!' The man answered, 'What a strange thing it is! You do not know where he comes from, but he cured me of my blindness! We know that God does not listen to sinners; he does listen to people who respect him and do what he wants them to do. Since the beginning of the world nobody has ever heard of anyone giving sight to a person born blind. Unless this man came from God, he would not be able to do a thing.' They answered, 'You were born and brought up in sin—and you are trying to teach us?' And they expelled him from the synagogue.

John 9:13–17, 24–34

If you want to read the full story and find out what this man's parents said look up John 9:13–34.

The suggestions are that Jesus could be a prophet, an ordinary man or the messiah. Write down the evidence from the passage which supports these three ideas:

A prophet . . . .

. . . .

An ordinary man . . . .

. . . .

The Messiah . . . .

. . . .

Jesus' power to perform miracles came from God. Jesus obeyed God and only did what his Father wanted him to do. The man who was healed realized this and said, 'Unless this man comes from God, he would not be able to do a thing.' If you investigate the life of Jesus you can see that he was no ordinary man. No one has had such power as Jesus. Yet he commanded no army and ruled no country. He never wrote a book or travelled very far. Yet his words influence millions. He was very special because he was sent by God to do God's work. But if Jesus was who he claimed to be, the one sent by God, then we cannot afford to ignore him. We must do as he says and obey his instructions.

The man who was healed by Jesus was very courageous. He stood up for Jesus even when under pressure from the religious authorities. We must also stand up for our belief in Jesus even when it is difficult and others do not share our views.

Dear Jesus, sometimes I take life for granted, sometimes I'm full of doubt, sometimes I find it difficult to cope. Yet in other countries there are Christians who suffer because they believe in you. Help me to follow their good example and to stand up for my faith in you. Amen.

24

Read John 9:35–41

I believe

When Jesus heard what had happened, he found the man and asked him, 'Do you believe in the Son of Man?' The man answered, 'Tell me who he is, sir, so that I can believe in him!' Jesus said to him, 'You have already seen him, and he is the one who is talking with you now.' 'I believe, Lord!' the man said, and knelt down before Jesus. Jesus said, 'I came to this world to judge, so that the blind should see and those who see should become blind.' Some Pharisees who were there with him heard him say this and asked him, 'Surely you don't mean that we are blind, too?' Jesus answered, 'If you were blind, then you would not be guilty; but since you claim that you can see, this means that you are still guilty.'

We all believe things that we cannot see. We may not have been to Rome or Moscow but we believe that they exist. We believe in gravity but we cannot see it. We all believe in electricity but we cannot point to it. We believe Rome or Moscow exist because of the evidence. We may have seen pictures of them or spoken to someone who has been there. We know gravity exists because we can see the effect. If we throw something up in the air it falls to earth

POOR CHAP – HE REFUSES TO BELIEVE IN GRAVITY AS HE CAN'T SEE IT !!

again. The same is true of electricity. You cannot see it but you can point to its effect. All you have to do is turn on the light switch.

We may not be so fortunate as the man who was healed from blindness. Something so dramatic may not have happened to us. But it does not mean that we cannot believe.

We need to investigate the facts and look at the evidence, and make up our own mind. Do you believe in God:

☐ Because of what the Bible says

☐ Because it is important to my family

☐ Because it is important to my friends

☐ Because God gives a purpose to my life and a reason for living

☐ Because I believe death is not the end

☐ Because of Jesus

Put a tick beside the ones that help you believe in God. You may tick one or all of them.

The man healed by Jesus knew that Jesus was someone special. He must be special otherwise he would not have the power to do miracles. He could now see with his eyes but he also had the power to see who Jesus was. He was able to see physically and spiritually.

The facts show us that Jesus was someone very special. What he said and did has had more influence on mankind than anyone else. Science may explain some of the questions of how life works but only God can show us the 'why' and the point to life.

Lord help me to see and believe. Let me know the truth of your love and power and show it to those around me. Amen.

25

The death of Lazarus

Take your Bible and turn to John 11:1–16.

One thing all of us can say for certain is that eventually each one of us will die. This is very sad but we cannot avoid it. It happens to everyone. However Jesus, by this miracle, wanted to show that death is not the end. In this passage Jesus says two things which seem to contradict each other. What are they? Write your answer down below, next to the two verses you need to look at:

verse 11 . . . .

verse 14 . . . .

Lazarus was dead but he was asleep. In other words he was physically dead but with God death is not the end. To demonstrate that, Jesus intended to bring Lazarus back to life. Jesus wants to bring glory to God—to show everyone what God is able to do. Not even death can limit the power of God. Nothing can limit his power.
When going on a journey you rely on two things—a map and signpost. Without these you would be lost. God gives us both a map and signposts, not just for life, but also for death. In the Bible we find instructions and 'signs' which point the way. This sign of raising Lazarus back to life is meant to show us that God's power can conquer even death. Jesus went on to show this by coming back from death himself.
What is the festival we celebrate which remembers this?

. . . .

We also remember this each week when, during the communion service, we all say, 'Christ has died, Christ is risen, Christ will come again.'

Dear Lord, help me to trust you day by day for the rest of my life on earth. Then when I am faced by death hold my hand and lead the way. For Jesus Christ's sake, who lived and died and rose again for us. Amen.

What a pro

Some promises you can rely on, others you cannot. With the list below write on a scale of 0–10 how reliable their promises are (0 = completely unreliable, 10 = completely reliable).

A TV commercial
0 1 2 3 4 5 6 7 8 9 10

A policeman
0 1 2 3 4 5 6 7 8 9 10

A car salesman
0 1 2 3 4 5 6 7 8 9 10

A politician
0 1 2 3 4 5 6 7 8 9 10

A newspaper advert
0 1 2 3 4 5 6 7 8 9 10

A vicar
0 1 2 3 4 5 6 7 8 9 10

A lawyer
0 1 2 3 4 5 6 7 8 9 10

A businessman
0 1 2 3 4 5 6 7 8 9 10

Your brother or sister
0 1 2 3 4 5 6 7 8 9 10

God
0 1 2 3 4 5 6 7 8 9 10

Something or someone may promise a great deal but you know that they will not keep their promise. Others you can rely on. When they say something will be done, it happens.

When God makes a promise it is a very serious matter and you can be completely confident that he will not break his promise.

Now look at the passage John 11:17–27. Read it carefully.

When Jesus arrived, he found that Lazarus had been buried four days before. Bethany was less than three kilometres from Jerusalem, and many Judeans had come to see Martha and Mary to comfort them over their brother's death. When Martha heard that Jesus was coming, she went out to meet him, but Mary stayed in the house. Martha said to Jesus, 'If you had been here, Lord, my brother would not have died! But I know that even now God will give you whatever you ask him for.' 'Your brother will rise to life,' Jesus told her. 'I know,' she replied, 'that he will rise to life on the last day.' Jesus said to her, 'I am the resurrection and the life. Whoever believes in me will live, even though he dies; and whoever lives and believes in me will never die. Do you believe this?' 'Yes, Lord!' she answered, 'I do believe that you are the Messiah, the Son of God, who was to come into the world.'

...mise!

In this passage there is a great promise. It comes in verse 25, where Jesus says, 'I am the resurrection and the life. Whoever believes in me will live, even though he dies; and whoever lives and believes in me will never die.'
The wonderful thing is that by trusting in Jesus he promises eternal life. That is life of eternal value. God will not let you down. He does not forget what he has said. Death will not be the end of everything. But no one can believe for you. Not your mum or dad, or grandparents.

You have to believe for yourself. That is why Jesus added, 'Do you believe this?' If you can answer 'Yes' for yourself, then you can confidently rely that God will keep his promise. But to say 'Yes' doesn't mean you may not have a lot of questions to which you are looking for an answer. You do not have to know all the answers before you say 'Yes'. It just means you recognize that God is bigger than your questions and he can be relied on.

Heavenly Father, thank you that you keep your promises. You have promised eternal life to those who believe in you. Thank you for the life you have given to me. Amen.

27

Collect together any old newspapers that you can find. Spread them out on the floor. Go through them and cut out any stories that make you feel sad. Then write down why they make you feel sad below.

. . . .

. . . .

. . . .

. . . .

LAZARUS IS DEAD!

BAD NEWS

In the story about Lazarus Jesus felt very sad, in fact the passage says he cried. He was upset at the bad news.

Mary arrived where Jesus was, and as soon as she saw him, she fell at his feet. 'Lord,' she said, 'if you had been here, my brother would not have died!' Jesus saw her weeping, and he saw how the people who were with her were weeping also; his heart was touched, and he was deeply moved. 'Where have you buried him?' he asked them. 'Come and see, Lord,' they answered. Jesus wept. 'See how much he loved him!' the people said. But some of them said, 'He gave sight to the blind man, didn't he?

Could he not have kept Lazarus from dying?'

John 11:32–37

God cares about you and me. He cares about the world he has made. But the only way he can change things is to use people who are prepared to listen and do good. Jesus is relying on us to show love to others.

During the last war many churches were damaged by the bombing from both sides. One particular church in Germany which had a magnificent

Love and compassion

statue of Jesus was virtually destroyed one night by bombs. When the war was over the people of that town decided to rebuild the church. One man who was a sculptor offered to repair the statue of Jesus which had also been damaged and was without any hands. The priest and the people met together to consider the offer but decided to leave the statue as it was. So today each time someone goes into the church they can see the statue without any hands and it reminds them that Jesus has no hands on earth today but our hands.

God cares about this world and each person in it. But he wants us to play our part to change the bad news into good and he has given us the power to do it. Now take the rest of the remaining newspapers and cut out the stories that make you feel happy. Then write down what is good about these stories below.

. . . .

. . . .

. . . .

. . . .

. . . .

Lord, make us instruments of your peace. Where there is hatred, let us bring love; where there is injury, pardon; where there is discord, union; where there is doubt, faith; where there is despair, hope; where there is darkness, light; where there is sadness, joy. For Jesus Christ's sake. Amen.

P.S. Place your hands on these two pages. Get someone to draw round them with a pen or pencil. Remember these hands of yours are the hands of Jesus.

GOOD NEWS

LAZARUS RAISED FROM THE DEAD

28

 Read John 11:38–44

Amazing

Deeply moved once more, Jesus went to the tomb, which was a cave with a stone placed at the entrance. 'Take the stone away!' Jesus ordered. Martha, the dead man's sister, answered, 'There will be a bad smell, Lord. He has been buried four days!' Jesus said to her, 'Didn't I tell you that you would see God's glory if you believed?' They took the stone away. Jesus looked up and said, 'I thank you Father, that you listen to me. I know that you will always listen to me, but I say this for the sake of the people here, so that they will believe you sent me.' After he had said this, he called out in a loud voice, 'Lazarus, come out!' He came out, his hands and feet wrapped in grave clothes, and with a cloth round his face. 'Untie him,' Jesus told them, 'and let him go.'

What is the most amazing sight that you have ever seen? Was it a firework display or a scene on holiday? Was it the view from the top of a mountain or the sight of an amazing animal? It could have been a scene at sea or a cave underground? What do you remember feeling when you saw that amazing sight? Did you shout for joy or were you quiet because it made you feel small?

Imagine that you were at the scene of Jesus bringing Lazarus back to life. Note down some of the things you imagine you would have felt seeing this amazing sight:

....

....

....

....

....

However Jesus showed by his own coming back to life that death is not the end.
That is why we should live our lives God's way.

If you had been standing there you would have heard Jesus speaking to his Father. What did he say that was so important. Write it down in the space below.

. . . .

. . . .

. . . .

. . . .

WOW!

God the Father listened to his son Jesus. But Jesus also listened to his Father. They worked together. Jesus raised Lazarus back to life because he loved Lazarus and because he wanted people to believe that God had sent him. And Jesus proved that by bringing Lazarus back to life. What an amazing sight. Jesus has the power over life and death.
Lazarus came back to life, but eventually he would have died again.

Lord of all life and power, who through the mighty resurrection of your Son overcame death, help us to us to live our lives in the power of your love both now and for all eternity.
Amen.

29

What next?

The *Following Jesus* Series

If you have enjoyed using *The Power of Jesus*, you might like to look at other titles in the series.

Following Jesus presents a lively and stimulating introduction to the Christian faith in words and cartoons. Suitable for use as a confirmation course, the 31 steps/units (with practical suggestions and prayers) cover the basics of Christian teaching and discipleship. An additional leaflet is available which provides leaders with suggestions for four weekly sermons. Price: £2.99 per copy (£25 for a pack of 10).

Serving Jesus tackles many of the questions and problems facing young people as they try to serve Jesus. A further 27 units are presented, each linked with a character or event from the New Testament and including a short Bible reading and prayer. *Serving Jesus* will be particularly suitable for those who have just been confirmed. Price: £1.95 per copy (£15 for a pack of 10).

Praying with Jesus presents 28 units which each explore one aspect of 'praying with Jesus', with a Bible reading, comment and short assignment. *Praying with Jesus* will appeal to confirmation and post-confirmation candidates and any person anxious to learn more about prayer. Price £1.95 per copy (£15 for a pack of 10). ʼ

Picturing Jesus contains 28 units which consider the seven 'I Am' sayings in John's Gospel—the pictures which Jesus used to illustrate and show who he was: 'I am the Good Shepherd', 'I am the Vine', 'I am the Bread of Life', 'I am the Way, the Truth and the Life', 'I am the Light of the World', 'I am the Resurrection and the Life', 'I am the Gate'. Price: £2.99 per copy (£25 for a pack of 10).

Another 7 titles are planned in the *Following Jesus* series.

All titles in the series are illustrated throughout by Taffy.

Following Jesus, Serving Jesus, Praying with Jesus and *Picturing Jesus* are available now from all good Christian Bookshops, or in case of difficulty from BRF, Peter's Way, Sandy Lane West, Oxford, OX4 5HG. If ordering direct from BRF please add 15% (minimum 85p) to cover post and packing.

If you would like to know more about the full range of Bible reading notes and other Bible reading group study materials published by the Bible Reading Fellowship, write and ask for a free catalogue.